Learn About Animals

Hen

By Cecilia Minden

This is a pen.

The hen is in the pen.

This is a hen.

The hen is in the nest.

This is a nest.

The eggs are in the nest.

This is a chick.

The chick is in the egg.

This is a chick.

The chick is in the nest.

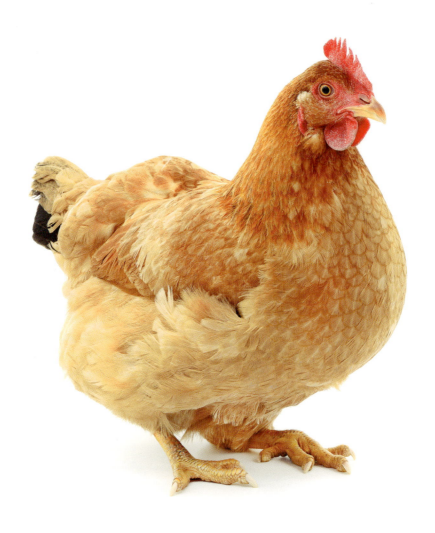

This is a hen.

The hen and chicks are in the nest.

Word List

sight words

a is
and The
are This

short e words

egg
eggs
hen
nest
pen

short i words

chick
chicks
in

62 Words

This is a pen.
The hen is in the pen.
This is a hen.
The hen is in the nest.
This is a nest.
The eggs are in the nest.
This is a chick.
The chick is in the egg.
This is a chick.
The chick is in the nest.
This is a hen.
The hen and chicks are in the nest.

Published in the United States of America by Cherry Lake Publishing
Ann Arbor, Michigan
www.cherrylakepublishing.com

Photo Credits: © Tsekhmister/Shutterstock.com, front cover, 1, 4, 12, 15; © Oleksandr Lytvynenko/Shutterstock.com, back cover, 10; © marilyn barbone/Shutterstock.com, 2; © Nannycz/Shutterstock.com, 3; © JFJacobsz/Shutterstock.com, 5; © Thieury/Shutterstock.com, 6; © Dharapong Tupjan/Shutterstock.com, 7; © Anneka/Shutterstock.com, 8, 9; © Nataly Studio/Shutterstock.com, 11; © Olga Samostrova/Shutterstock.com, 13

Copyright © 2018 by Cherry Lake Publishing

All rights reserved. No part of this book may be reproduced or utilized
in any form or by any means without written permission from the publisher.

Cherry Blossom Press is an imprint of Cherry Lake Publishing.

Library of Congress Cataloging-in-Publication Data

Names: Minden, Cecilia, author.
Title: Hen / by Cecilia Minden.
Description: Ann Arbor : Cherry Lake Publishing, [2018] | Series: Learn about animals |
    Audience: Grade pre-school, excluding K. | Includes index.
Identifiers: LCCN 2017031594| ISBN 9781534123977 (pbk.) | ISBN 9781534123854 (pdf) |
    ISBN 9781534124097 (hosted ebook)
Subjects: LCSH: Chickens–Juvenile literature. | Readers (Primary) | Reading–Phonetic method.
Classification: LCC SF487.5 .M57 2018 | DDC 636.5–dc23
LC record available at https://lccn.loc.gov/2017031594

Printed in the United States of America
Corporate Graphics

Cecilia Minden is the former director of the Language and Literacy Program at Harvard Graduate School of Education. She earned her PhD in Reading Education at the University of Virginia. Dr. Minden has written extensively for early readers. She is passionate about matching children to the very book they need to improve their skills and progress to a deeper understanding of all the wonder books can hold. Dr. Minden and her family live in McKinney, Texas.